BEETHOVEN AND THE BIRDS

Beethoven and the Birds

poems

Judith Skillman

BLUE BEGONIA PRESS • YAKIMA WA

Grateful acknowledgment is made to the following publications in which these poems first appeared, some in different versions:

Northwest Review, "The Violin Mark," "Under the Glass Counter,"
    "Oodles of Tiny Fiddles," "To See Shadows," "A Bouquet
    for the Sleepless," "The Problem of a Horse without
    Water," "Amnesia," "Complicity," "A Conceit," "Seepage"
Willow Springs, "Dvorak's Childhood," "Under Zeus"
Southern Humanities Review, "The Fingerboard"
Journal of the American Medical Association, "Tinnitus," "Case
    History," "Bubba"
Southern Poetry Review, "The Strads"
Exhibition, "Whole Note"
Fine Madness, "Summering," "The Birdwomen Discuss Ugly
    Beauty," "Mother's Cooking," "The Inchworm"
Laurel Review, "The Night Nurse"
Poetry Northwest, "Gourds," "The Queen of Fatigue,"
    "Improvisations for Echo"
Iowa Review, "The Housewife Dreams of Order," "Harbor Song"
Fever Dreams, "Fugue State"
Malahat Review, "The Woman Who Thinks She Is Me"
Midwest Quarterly, "Mist," "In the Parlor of Elliptical Billiards"
Poet and Critic, "Hamilton Street"
Nightsun, "Wasp's Nest"
Silverfish Review, "Nine Years Without Music," "An Anarchy"
Seneca Review, "The Bird in the Attic Window"
Iris, "Midday"
Southern Review, "The Vagaries of Fishes"

My thanks to Linda Andrews, Christianne Balk, Beth Bentley, Barbara Molloy-Olund, and Carolyn Willis.

Cover painting and division page illustrations by Priscilla Maynard.
Book design by Karen and Jim Bodeen.
ISBN 0-911287-19-1

Blue Begonia Press   225 S. 15th Ave   Yakima, WA 98902-3821

For Tom, Lisa, Drew, and Jocelyn

Not a lullaby,-- Gong! Gong!
What casts a spell over other gods
lets this most cunning god escape
into his ever-receding power.

Rilke, "Idol," *Uncollected Poems*

TABLE OF CONTENTS

1. FILO

2. FUGUE

3. WHOLE NOTE

1. Filo

A CONCEIT

While doing laundry
a woman finds a fragment of music
stuck like pitch
to a shirt, and begins to swab
in circles with her bristly brush,
but the pitch is stubborn--
it coats her hands.

When she goes to wash them
she finds herself
rooted to the floor
like a willow, utterly graceful,
her hands welded
to bronze faucets.

She notices dark wings
brushing against her face--
the hair of a younger woman,
but who?
If she could turn her head
she is certain she would recognize
the figure.

Deep in the recesses of her shoulders
she feels warmth, and now the sun
has broken through the window
as though it too
wants to return her
to her life.

CASE HISTORY

A toppled tree.
I can see where water
softened its roots
until they gave way.

This tree reminds me of a strong woman
who does for others.
Even now she lies
like a patient full of trust
in a green hospital.

Snow melts,
trickles down foothills.
One by one the white doctors
come to the foot of her bed,
tired from the effort
it takes not to care.
They thumb pages
and whisper to each other.

I imagine they are sewing her up,
stitching her midriff
back together with beaks and feathers.
That they have conferred
and discovered contagion,
or worse.

It's so quiet I can hear
my thoughts falling around me.
The hush of a library,
or that place in a story
where something wants to happen.

Skunk grass, poison weed, and nettles conspire.
Yellow fungus blooms
on a log, and I remember
four hollow tubes carrying waste
from its endless site.

I think the patient
wants to die
but doesn't know how.
So she lies there
facing the sky,
dirt forming a black skirt
around her legs.

FILO

Fresh-cut quills fingered
by a dreary light, the same
that unwraps Constanze
from her restless, pre-dawn dreams.
Before bed he wrote to his father:
death is the key which unlocks the door
to our true happiness.

Then insomnia, the indiscriminate guest.
Fragments and incipits strewn around the room
on scraps, the old aria of the English Bach
still ringing in his ears,
he cups his head in his hands
and sees a simpler line,
written in an ink
that thickens quickly.
Varicolored shades of peacock
and persimmon peel back
from stems of notes several seeded
on brown paper.

Strands of his sleeping wife's hair
tangle. Come morning
she will be fashionable again,
the problems solved,
even this childhood riddle from the Orient:
the sum a petty chess player received
from the King.

Then the finale of Don Giovanni, written
as one writes a letter.

TINNITUS

All night the woman floats
in her twin bed, hearing the wind
whoosh, the rain slap and beat
against shutters. She has given
everything to find this white river,
where she can stand and see the glacier
move its snout along a ridge, nosing
the ground as it uproots trees
and sends rocks to their death.

But rocks can't die, she thinks,
as wind and rain pour ceaselessly
through her. She supposes the past, like matter,
can be neither created nor destroyed.
And as she sleeps she rummages
through shells on a beach, touching feathers
that murmur like birds, looking
for her lost ring. In her dream she hears
the common crow chase a red-tailed hawk
into a corner of the sky.

Beside her bed the ocean roars
its single name, coursing
from the sound conditioner.
A light rain thrums. Wind choruses
its white noise, wakening
vibrations deep within her cochleae.
She hears her mother's fine china
shiver from a shelf and break.

WASP'S NEST

What of these paper rooms,
three tiers rising
from a fallen log
that's nursed a few poor trees
to adolescence.

I pass by, peer close. Inside the hotel
no one's talking. An anarchy
of silence has moved in
where once wasps lived,
bumping out messages against the walls.

I see moss creeping closer,
feel the touch of scalloped fungi
against deadwood.
Rusty music trickles from a creek.
This is mid-life,

grown babies folded into photographs,
hoarding their stocky bodies
for the next generation.
An undisclosed ache
takes liberties with a joint.

Dry needles sift from fir trees.
Inside one of the hundred rooms
the shell of a fellow conspirator
huddles, its stinger bent
like a symbol from an old alphabet.

AN ANARCHY

Even vacant the wasp's nest
presents its small shock
to the forest--a paper hotel
with endless rooms.

Inside it's quiet.
The wasps aren't policing our picnic,
so the offering, a thigh or a wing,
isn't necessary. Summer already
gone, a few wildflowers
feign heartiness. Inside the hollow
pause. Under the upstairs guests.
Someone pacing back and forth.

Cigarettes, and the scent of a tree
cut up into logs.
Later the sawdust, the queries, the afternoon.
No one's talking. Not the telephone,
which was made for petty inquiries
but has lately fallen silent.
That comrade's incommunicado.

Death the editor.
Room upon room.
Floors that give, walls stained
with scallops of moisture.

OODLES OF TINY FIDDLES

They grow in rows.
I have to concentrate to see them,
first flowers, prim with the winter sun
on their necks and backs,
their ebony stems sleek.

I am unwrapping some remnant
of fear so raw it threatens to disappear.
Violins instead of flowers--
how perfectly they break ground,
like the first sharp blades of crocus.

This must be the key signature of the child:
versions, copies, imitations,
the sturdy wood
of first failure.

Like leftover child selves
they flood the garden
in need of tending,
bursting through leaves and mulch.

I finger their shy scrolls
and frosted fingerboards.
Is it dangerous to imagine
these rows and columns of wooden girls
with perfect figures?

How polite they are,
still slightly damp
from birth, frosted with lines of purfling,
delivered from their waxy cheesecloth

by the air.
When the winter sun sets like a lump of rosin
I'll go out with my broom
and begin the song of sweeping
close to their red and blonde heads.
Stiff petals, mute trumpets,

I'll thread a needle,
tighten a screw, pluck my own guts
in order to sew them
one to the other--these little selves
that equal a whole:
the eighth, quarter, half, three-quarter.

NINE YEARS WITHOUT MUSIC

Even so the daffodils grow straight up
toward the ceiling
in their clay pot,
bulbs half bared.

They cast fantastic shadows
that play against drawn curtains.

You are glad to have retired
to your stiff bed, grateful
for the half-grown child
who sleeps in the dark now.

The sheets are peppered
with fragments of flowers and ducks.
Rain sifts through the leaves
that are left, making small
hissing sounds.

Your younger sister is gone.
So there is no one to harmonize with,
to take the lower part
or besiege you with questions.
Only the dull arms of other women
who have tried to fill in, like trees,
the utterance.

Wearing black to a party
you seem not to be in mourning,
as the scallops wince in their bacon wraps.
Voices waft past you,

part of the background
and therefore a kind of answer,
like fatigue, or annoyance.

Already the days are getting longer
as you stand there,
just a hair outside your own body
without seeming to notice
the blurring of boundaries.

UNDER THE GLASS COUNTER

I remember powdered sugar rose from angel wings,
delicate pastries brushed with yolk
and shaped in figure eights.

The sugar blurs
and I'm tired. An infinity
has passed; why must I stand
like a child in this shop
of thick accents, and watch my grandmother
tend her heavy pot of knaidlach and pipicle--
lumpy snowballs in a broth
flavored with the bellybuttons of chickens?

I understand she has no charwoman
to help at home, that she will get a back alley abortion
this afternoon, at the same hour
my youngest daughter returns home from school
and kicks in the door,
wanting to be older.

The pastries are tough
as leather, or maybe the years
have turned them into decorations.
Fresh versions sit on trays in the back room
where a new crop of bakers,
hired yesterday, stands and chats,
making small talk,
little words that nourish
when it's too hot to eat.

I know powdered sugar only seems to rise,
that nothing has changed

under glass. Neither dust
nor snow blankets the small triangles, circles,
and squares
bearing long-voweled names I learned
with the ease of a child:
hamentaschen, kugel, rogeleh.

So nothing intervenes
to make my standing here like a midget
in my grandparents' store on the seedy side of Montreal
more or less like history.

SEEPAGE

In a little while we will be free.
In a short time the birds will leave
their estuary of songs
about salmon lying belly up
in a stream. It departs,

little by little, the body's allotment
of blood. From this one might deduce
that a woman has been bled,
that her rubber breasts
are all that remain of fright.

It gets worse. Anxiety breeds
small crises, in the backlit trees
layered like dry brush
upon the sky, in paper silhouettes
of other birds placed at the fork

of the tree. Their needle-nose beaks.
So I call up a friend and implicate
myself this time of month,
not a confession
exactly, but the self taking

a scaffold down. What my friend calls
"self talk," bubbling to the surface
in black veils of grease, corrosive
as the white fish drawn in chalk
over a storm sewer. Always fixing

on the next thing to ruin--
a plate of cake falling in slow motion

to the floor, and then this sweeping
it all up, as if nothing ever happened.
So whatever trauma is

it goes on stalking us on a wet day
if we are intent on the task
of containment. The incident
that draws me to its heart
like a secret garden is always here

and I am the one who must
keep the essential third part
of arterial blood inside,
in the body's black rivers,
until it forfeits its right to mysterious causes.

BEETHOVEN AND THE BIRDS

Walking from the lukewarm waters of the Danube
to a small door cut in history
he pauses near handfuls of tiny birds
set like bombs in the bushes and trees
bordering the baths.

                         Opening
the door because now they are reduced
to notes he can't hear over the buzzing
of his own ears.

Verbless birds.
Husked notes.
Skeletal birds,
birds of procrastination,
song of the loneliness of many women
not yet translated into one...

The sight of yellow and red bars,
green bellies moot against the bark
of winter trees stops him short.

And no, this never happened.
There were no birds of this ilk near the Danube.
His home away from home
was less private than a trail I walk
afternoons, cedar swath
set back from substantial houses.

                 His bear shape wanders off
on a tangential path with slow, unhurried power
and I climb into bed between layers of flannel,
not wanting to hear anymore.

BUBBA

In recollection
she's grown bulky, I suppose.
That's why she won't go upstairs
to the second-story room
full of mothballs and red beads,
the outgrown dresses whispering
on long racks.

Sometimes I hear baby woodpeckers squawk from trees.
I think they were abandoned
in conifers,
born and then forgotten,
but it's possible even these unfortunates
are protected
because of her, kept from the evil eye
thanks to a bit of sputum
frozen to a leaf.

Her grave's more shallow
than it was years ago.
Her corpse is a nurse log
with squatter's rights,
lying on its side
in the great woods.

If I walk on solid mud
past her head
stuck in the ground
like a winter cabbage,
who will stop me?

Her right to sit up late
reading the endless Agatha Christies

translated into Polish,
laughing out loud,
strategizing
and talking to herself.

I suppose she's busy bargaining with God,
entertaining him
with fancy causes and effects.
I can still hear her arguments ebb and flow
in sickness, see her orange blood,
arterial, in the soft wood
of fallen cedars.

I know blood is black
when it comes from the stomach,
and bright red when it stems
from lower down. I've learned
that there are as many germs
in the body as there are citizens
of the earth.

Having heard enough already,
she brings the cataracts
of her cloudy eyes
close to my face.

THE FINGERBOARD

Inside the circle
of my hand are hermits
with lifted pincers.
Their borrowed
houses blacken.

A secret,
the ebony gives.
Under the new
order there's a rush
on glass figurines.
When I crush them
I hear the pop of gristle,
sound of a broken nose
or a statistician
counting the odds.
I can't believe how tiny
the numbers, how delicate.

And this is only a sampling
of superstructures
it took centuries to build.
I coax shellfish
out of the middle ear.

One doctor reported
cutting through bone stays
with a knife, to release
the hordes of ladies
who fainted in public.

I stomp
the exact center

of each note
in order to approach
even one of the deformed angels
with its fear
of flowers and numbers.

AMNESIA

Give in to your fatigue. It's good for you
to lie face down on the flowered bedspread
breathing in sharpened points of petals, or stars.

Give in and go deeply inward,
past the machines with their vibrato,
under a canopy of daylight and the ministering
hands of the big leaf maple. With no map
or water glass, without a doubt
or a reason. You've already forgotten the part
about being born, and the story of you as a child.

And after the street has been taken apart, it will be torn
and patched, rusty wires re-routed, replaced.
In your head there will be merely the sensation
of counting. Benign snakes will lie between cracks
sunning themselves, and maybe the lizard will move away
from a shadow, its outgrown skins
wadded here and there, like gunny sacks.
You might lie for hours head first
as though pinned to the second half of your life

while daylight traces leaves on the ground
and lethargic birds stretch their claws away from branches
of the tree that scrapes against the house
during windstorms, with a human sound.

2. Fugue

THE HOUSEWIFE DREAMS OF ORDER

They say a spray of lavender
hung upside down in a closet,
they say lemons. But she
knows better. She lets

the old screen off its hook
and stands clear. There,
it is morning. It is morning,
and noontime, and evening again

yet she has not moved.
She is planted squarely
in the space of their comings
and goings, she is waxen

and broad leafed, her shoulder
blades oiled as a fine wood,
her mind swept clean.
Nothing moves in her, no

shadows upon the triangle
of her throat and neck,
no kerchief. The wind is a rosin
that plays her hair.

THE QUEEN OF FATIGUE

I wasn't feeling anything when the queen
of fatigue began her dance of tercets, reeling me
in like a big fish on a spinner. She was decked out

in ribbons that curled of their own volition--
no shears opening and closing the shark's noncommittal
grin, no blade held over the scene of gift-giving.

No, she was just what the doctor ordered: plenty
of rest, knowing full well that rest doesn't equal
sleep; that the dreams of those who can't lose consciousness

begin in the full light of a kitchen, and gradually
take on color, mystery, what-you-will, deepening
to hallucination. I wasn't averse to her presence, just

feeling my way between the boulders of moments when she
happened to be, as if by her being exact enough
I'd later think to replicate her studded face, her blue garters stocked

with big and little fish–those we used to consider too small
to keep, too large to throw back without regret. Her face had been
leeched by crystals of rock salt. Her blush taken from a stone.

She didn't speak except as the cheap trick of a painter
who stoops to get the impression of frost, bare as paper,
against the broken window pane of a barn. Her legs were

twice lovely, plump and sinewy as egrets. A kingfisher
defined the way her collarbone stood out from her neck,
bent like a bow, primed to dive. As I wasn't doing anything

to keep her at arm's length, to this day she hides
between chinks in the dock, declares her ownership
over poles that light my path, each lamp a gull

bright enough to lose its shadow to midday sun.

COMPLICITY

It is sad to be tired, to see
my mother opening draperies
on a square of yard. The stars
grind to a halt and the kitchen
begins to hum. I've left my body

sleepless on the bed in the study
and risen to greet her
on her rounds:
coffee ground fresh
and oranges halved and pressed
until their seeds loosen
like delicate slivers.

I've been up all night
waiting for her to begin
these rituals
she composes for no one.

Her strange eyes are black like a bird's
and she turns her head
around to see behind her
but she can't help me this time.
I'm watching the quiet hour
before morning begins in earnest.

It's uncomfortable to be up this early,
so close to her odd way
of making do.
I see the buttons of her teeth
and the robe as old as memory,
a common shift of seersucker.

Sure of nothing
she stands there, friable
in dawn's sleazy light
above the whisper
of a pilot light so happy to be lit,
on the morning she first decided
to let me see how fragile she was.

THE BIRD IN THE ATTIC WINDOW

In the mind of the quilt maker
all things can be divided,
the foreign bird clasping
its second branch in crooked hands,

the pasture land beyond
a list of silos, an echo complete.
The symbol for flower,
whispered again, becomes a heart

or a star. The frame we desire
contains a sill so deep
that to lean into it
is to grasp softness

with our arms, or else
fall. To obtain these effects
a woman has purchased
the same bird many times,

she has notched its beak
into tissue with a wheel of teeth,
and backed out of her dreams
in order to leave the bird whole,

listening awake to its refusals,
seeing its clothing of feathers.
She would be happy
to stroke its head

before the fire, after
her cooking is finished,

when the blueberries have been
transplanted from one cold spot

to another.
The knots that hold her, *war-bride,*
bag-balm, are just tokens,
but there is no better rest,

no better place to lay her damaged hands.

THE STRADS

There, on the rooftop, the seccadour
waits for summer in all its versions,
for first wife Francesca
to lift a string of dates
and simultaneously bear him an infant,
already swaddled, wound in a square
of blue silk, mewing at her breast
like a Persian cat.

Linen stiffens to brocade
and figs adorn the walls, pear-shaped trifles
like his newest violins, hung up to dry
alongside her pummeled shirts and fruits.

Suppose Francesca sings a nursery rhyme.
Does she dare to sing there,
in the great house?

*

Their still life as seen through a narrow window
half a year later: a few marginal notes of snow
sift through trestles. No wind. Where the snow collects,
it blues, like breast milk.

She glances down,
toward the south with its sultry islands
from her vantage point four stories high,
the baby sandwiched between her breasts,
its stocky arms and legs.
She knows how to coax it back to sleep
by holding it just so.

*

The violin lies in a velvet coffin,
the French side of the family,
copy of a Claude Pierray, proch la Comedie.
Built in Paris, 1725, a fraud.

The family heirloom, abandoned when a sister's wrists ached,
her hands grew numb. Dormant now,
uncomplaining, a sometime stowaway and product of neglect.

The wood swells
each Parisian summer, hairline cracks opening seams
under a light dusting of rosin. Plum blossoms
fallen, changed by accretion
to winter drifts.

*

Like mother-of-pearl, winter light enters the shop downstairs
with the same free play of nuance,
with scarcely any departure from the norm.

Winter correctly begins here, in Milan,
where a patron buzzes in the back room,
poring over maps.

The cobblestone streets allow for a kind of traffic,
the stone-bruised horses blinded,
carrying heavy carriages, the perfectly exacted, massed choir
of crows settling into branches.

Suppose the rippling of boughs
stops, and night fills in the rest of the puzzle,

trees seamed and zipped together, an augury
for the simple flush-glued joints of the violin,
which can, in an emergency,
be re-opened. The inquest hasn't begun yet,

the instrument hasn't fallen silent, been housed in a museum
in a dust-free case, or altered
on a whim--fragile bow
speared at the frog, impaled by a ribbon of horsehair,
no longer dragged across a cake of resin.

*

What if even the *purfling*--
narrow inlay that follows the outline of edges
like the deeply walled townships,
what if this boundary
also functions. Keeps incipient splits
from growing across the violin's gracious belly and arched back.

*

The woodworm bores into the scroll after a century
or two, its path curving like a sickle,
leaving a sonorous darkness
where its body was,
a shell where its nakedness
grew teeth and metabolized maple.

One concave curl
tells of adjustments and thicknesses, layers
that absorb concussion a thousand-fold while resisting
the amateur. An instrument of torture.
A gigue wafts through open windows, as,

gardyloo, a wide-girthed servant
empties waste from a chamber pot--its trajectory
an arc, the stem of a flower
taken from a fold in the street
that fertilized the Black Plague.

*

Cremona.
On this reticent night,
with scarcely a deviation
from the norm, dusk light cools
to complement the warm wood,
it strikes back and frontispieces
lying face up on smooth tables
where the trio--a father and two sons, works.

From teardrop leaves of ficus
jays plunge, plangent shadows that carry off whole peanuts
in their beaks.

Francesca's wandering Jew thickens,
she waters the scrawling mass.
(Does she hum a bar or two from a music not yet composed?)

Each petal turns toward casts and bandages of light
falling through stained glass windows, each leaf
grows succulent as another false label.
Imitation! As if we were born again,
became our own children,
to add to our mother's delight.

Upstairs, in her draped bed,
Stradivarius' first and best wife turns over--the infant,

a tiny girl, fastened
to her hollows.

MIST

It emanates from plowed rows
of a field whose vanishing point
dissolves just beyond
a horse too white for detail.

So much light has lately shone on the picket fence
that it too is awash, though necessary
to the handsome buildings beyond.

Distortion allows the road to sweep
through flood plain as though it were
a tidal estuary. The birds
are forms. They flatter one another
as they shove beaks into the earth
for seed. A distant cove
finds its way beyond the cropped edges
of the scene. We can assume that sun
is slanting there as well,
burning off a wet-in-wet place
where dampness exists
for the sake of another chance
to paint reflections.

If our edges were less brittle,
the lines defining our roads
less broken by figures who stand
against fences to draw us in,
then we might stop the car,
get out and walk through cattails and Davy's gray
toward the furrows.

This might be called entering the picture,

an exercise schoolchildren do so carefully
that the last one is not caught
in a fast-failing light.

THE VAGARIES OF FISHES

After they passed beneath us I could tell
more would be coming, beneath the sand,
under the bejeweled sky, under the first
layer of earth where water exists
in flutes and eddies. I lay there with you,
not wanting to leave your side even
for them, the miraculous creatures of sex
and sediment, the ones who obey currents
and ladders, blindly seeking out their own
individual deaths, their pink flesh peeling
against the rocks. I saw the spool of eggs,
endless possibilities that would not be.
How they labored to breathe the air that night,
caught under our queen-sized bed, the male
and the female, Silvers and Kings whose pale
eyes saw into the lidless dark. I could tell
they loved each other without speech, circling
there apart from water, and I remembered
a snippet from a French film in which a woman
masturbates with a fish, and thought how progressive
I had become in retrospect. There we were,
left behind by the tides, deserted by
the institution of wind on a night
so soundless it could have been our first
night together, before we became victims
of those slippery, dirty, messy words.

FUGUE STATE

My mother stands at the window
cutting carrot roses.
Framed by the severe light
of another Syracuse winter,
she sings a tiny opera
of wrong notes.

After she's sung for an hour
with her mouth full of gold,
she measures water.

*

1954. Though only an infant
I enter the privacy of an argument
that takes place in Yiddish, words
whose sharps and flats
begin to sound.

The evil eye is the eye of a codfish,
a dislocated story
that makes its way around the table.

*

Mother heaps new potatoes on the table
and pares skins toward herself,
absently dipping the tool into flesh.
*If wishes were horses then beggars
would ride, a watched pot never boils,
it's no use crying over spilt milk.*

She stands at the stove,
her head in a cloud of steam.
She cuts the same flower many times
from the center of a carrot.

*

Remembering her face
is like staring at the sun.
I could believe I'm born again,

birthed by Mother and the cleaning lady
in a cubicle. No father, no doctor,
just me and Mother.
I cry and gulp air like a fish,
and she smiles her Pollyanna smile.
We live at the dawn of penicillin,
in a narrow barracks perched at the edge
of a university, or a war.

I'm five. Mother's wringer washer
inhales another shirt.
She wears the bloody apron of a butcher.
The days grow shorter. When all the food is gone
we will live on her proverbs.

WITHOUT CEREMONY

In two weeks nothing will change
except this currant bush tinged with blossoms
and acidic fruits. It's about to become a shield
for the burnt husk of an old-growth cedar.

You'll pick up your want ads and call
about another horse.
I can picture a thoroughbred straight from the track
nuzzling grain and alfalfa,
drinking from a chipped porcelain bathtub.

In two weeks nothing will change
but the moon, swollen like viscera,
plural as an organ the body doesn't know it has yet.

A slender girl,
you'll stand at dusk, with your hard breasts
and flat stomach, and I won't give this
poem to you, or listen to you recite
Hebrew words in a place beyond nerves.

Instead I'll wrap something pretty
and put it into your hands.
The animal you love will stare full on
at what it can see:
two peripheral scenes
cut by a dark swath down the middle.

THE WOMAN WHO THINKS SHE IS ME

Bares her elongated silhouette
in my distorted mirror.
Her children play
uphill at the stream's edge,
non-believers.
The mirror that distorts me
flatters her,
elongates the V of her neck.
Her dark lipsticks
grow like cattails
beside a flood plain.

The woman who usurps me
is not as beautiful as she imagines,
though, like me, she can't sleep.
The theorems which would prove
or disprove her existence
have faded, steam droplets
of the cloud which emanates
from my morning shower--
those rituals where she
lifts her breasts
and rinses the darkness
beneath each shallow world.

She can do her eyes two ways:
plum shadow or violet frost.
The circles of insomnia dusted
until they blend in.
Infinitesimal lines fan across
her cheekbones--pampas grass

or candelabra. Now the woman
who thinks only one thought
steps into the closet behind me
where the light is opening
its hands. She puts on my old arms

and outgrown belly.
She whispers invitations,
leads me toward
lid colors of midnight blue,
highlights of stardust pink--
until I am willing.
I enter her completely
as pockets in fields,
those which contain sheep
or chattel.

MOTHER'S COOKING

She's left the fish's head on
so it will bake slowly in foil, its milk eye
turning on finally like a light, its cheeks
growing tender.

She's come again to my house where the bowl
cats drink from is yellow with brine, and as if
that weren't bad enough she's taken over
my wire whisk, the one

with one bad arc. Beneath her cool hands
the boiling point of water lowers, bubbles shifting
from small to big so effortlessly
that when we watch the pot

it seems to stare back at us, concentrated
like the light that shone from her face
as I remember it. A few bananas go bad
in a basket that once held flowers, gaining

their spots gradually like an animal
I can't name, one she can't resist doing
something with. This will take up half the day,
as crowns of sugar and flour

bare their canisters, and the sun
wanes under her surprising
influence. Never measuring anything,
but tasting as she goes, as if she knows

how much more the sum will be,
how weak the parts in their estimation

of her powerful canon, she dominates
without opinion all the secrets

that are left of the world: rivers
flowing with the hearts of nuts, a land
bereft of butchers, and the last chicken
seen wearing feathers a woman will pluck.

IMPROVISATIONS FOR ECHO

"Come!"
"Come!"
"Why do you avoid me?"
"Why do you avoid me?"

Robert Graves, *Greek Myths I,"Narcissus"*

I would gather her into my arms
like a child, if she were not spent.
A breeze moves the arms of the great trees
and pools continue to form
across our path, puddles full of mallard couples.

What does she lack,
beside a lake called *Tradition*
in the late evening sun? I want to hold the last syllables
of our latest conversation like baubles,
in the tensile grip of her leafy fingers.
If you were Narcissus
I would hang, like her, on your words.

Among the deserving
she is a fate, her lithe body a string,
set to play music, in a cabin in the woods,
while the bees drill their honeycombs
and a man from the past
steps out of shadow.

In the company of strangers
she is an accomplice, her shyness
a prelude to mortification, her rites of stealth
laced like salt around the rim of a glass.

Widow tears. The speech of a woman
from a cold climate, talking of minks.

Distillation is her specialty:
an apron of needles spreading
across the lap of a forest,
a mannequin who sits
among false women,
her strapless dresses
hanging off their shoulders.

The corollary of her story
might be another life,
where we recollect ourselves
and discover we have lost our voices
deservedly, for aiding and abetting
the accomplices of the gods.

Adultery is not such a long way off.
Wood nymphs coalesce at the base of trees
with their thorn fingers,
and yellow flowers grow
like a blight. We call this beauty,

this time of year, and pledge ourselves
to our lawns, and to shadows--
flutes of trucks, long underbellies
of bird, and her jewelry
falling all day from the trees.

Once I lost my voice for you
but you bled to death anyway,
pressed to your own image
beside a pool of deepening pain.

My monosyllables were a punishment,
like hers, if there are no accidents,

if Echo is steeping again
in fancy bouquets, rigid
as sound, compulsive as a housewife.

MY PETITE VIOLIN

Sometimes I think she was given to me
by a sister whose wrists were damaged
by playing etudes in small rooms above an industrial city.
At other moments she's only an icon,
demure and tactful,
resting in her case.

The wood contracts--it shrinks
in winter and grows plump in summer.
But her joints are cushioned with invisible glue.
She's like a boat on the water,
forever ready to give and take.
Whatever problems she has are not mine,
the temperamental buzz or intermittent dullness.

I'll hold onto her as long as I can,
until my sister asks for her back
or we need the money she will bring
to feed our children. Until the war comes
so close to our house we can no longer
pretend it is only words. Her dormant hunger
is my joy, and her quirkiness makes me sad.

She has infiltrated my life at a tremendous price,
it's she I work for no matter what I do:
housecleaning, dressing, bathing.
If this seems to border on obsession,
I'll grow small, but don't mistake
this trim figure for the expression of the meek.

HARBOR SONG

The woman who stands with squid
behind her purse and the men
who stand with their curved
fishing poles, casting their hooks
upon a gesso reflection of sunset

all as essential as water.
The tugs that maneuver the flat boat
into shore and the rays of sun which appear
to diverge but are in fact parallel
and the ferries without lifeboats,
and the woman who stands with purse and squid

all of them as essential as water.
The sculpture of Christopher Columbus
and the drunk sleeping on his hook
in the wall, not so much a man
as an apparition, and the recessed
aquarium where at wrong angles
some tourists stand and stare, their curved
mouths like hooks descending

all of it as essential as water.
The meal we had, and the ferries
that did not tilt as the sun fell further
toward sunset, casting parallel rays
which we took to be slanted

all as essential as water.
The homeless, walking along pilings
that stand half exposed, black threading
whitecaps, and the woman and man

who fished away from us while I clutched
my purse, the catch they hid from us
while the optical illusion
of the sun died away

all of it as essential as water.

3. Whole Note

A SUMMER NIGHT

Cicadas cling in frozen postures
to the limbs
of deciduous trees.
An azalea steals light
from the full moon.
No one says how ghostly
it is to be left alone
upon the earth,
separated from the house
by a distance
of some five yards.
If this is Maryland,
then it must be the past.
Soon the cricket in my pocket
will start to fiddle,
taking up its bow
as stiff and dry as tinder.
The moon will shrink
and rise higher,
towards the stars.
I'll return to the house,
shoulder open
the unlocked door.
Inside I'll climb twelve stairs,
one for each year
I lived as a child,
and fall back
into the unmade bed
to wrap and unwrap
a plain white sheet
around my humid body.

DVORAK'S CHILDHOOD

Weekdays the sun falls on yellow leaves
lying in the yard. It warms them
and they tingle all over
like starfish,
like the hands of an audience.

I'm at the center of attention again;
my parents clap when I dance
to Ravel. Dvorak's childhood
plays out gradually through a stiff bow:
the rashes, the enforced isolation

and clear broth. At the sanitarium
he begins to eat again,
but his mother is weak
from sitting up nights next to his sickbed.
She takes longer to get well.

I'm gnawing at the string
with the frog of the bow, but I don't understand
anything yet. Not the years
welling up inside, or the way
my own mother sang out of tune,

blood and juice on her apron.
Soon the week will be over
and we'll be trapped here again
with one another: the children, the chores,
the simple leaves covering and uncovering the ground.

THE NIGHT NURSE

I'm in love with the night nurse.
We walk the floors together,
me barefoot, and her
wearing soft-soled shoes
that fluoresce beneath violent lights.

It goes without saying
that neither of us can sleep,
although she doesn't know how to drop off
and I am paid to milk the city
of its debts. I adore her impish face,
her curls plastered in a wet cap
over that mind that went wrong
when it twisted away from a fish.
I'm in love with the flowers
she brings, terra cotta centers
and reds so bright it's like seeing
my own blood for a second time.

She often runs out of containers
for these gifts
and has to hunt through drawers
until the odd-shaped urinal
surfaces. We are two of a kind,

I say, citing the way her mind works
on a problem I've given her
for which there is no answer,
only the dumb numbers circumnavigating
in their shells, divining the space
below the curve of her hips,
which will not end

when morning comes.
Beneath Teflon white
the spheres of her breasts
shine, and I tell her
we will be awake forever,
me pawing her with burning eyes,
her making me jealous
by dealing with daylight in a darkened room
miles from here.

A BOUQUET FOR THE SLEEPLESS

All night the uplifted stems
bear flowers. All winter,
all summer. They bloom
with or without water.
The ones tinged pink
will stay that way,
and the white
will stay white as a laundry
the housewife bleaches.
Baby's Breath--
each little rosette
composing its own history
for the bedroom mirror.
An empty glass,
a collection of florets
on a rod, endlessly repeating,
each time smaller,
more perfect.

THE INCHWORM

The inchworm is in charge of Spring,
hired by an underling
to make sure it all comes off according to plan.

But who is lower than the inchworm?
Every thirty feet another grub
clings to my cheek my hair my shirt...
What other scrap of silk
could keep us here on earth.

IN THE PARLOR OF ELLIPTICAL BILLIARDS

1. The Balls

Solid as ivory,
weighted as heavily as the heads
of sleeping children.

They glance off anything:
string, puddle walls, dishes the astronomers use
to collect their odds.

In my son's repetitive dream
the hallway is a pocket. It swallows him.
A dipper tapers in the small window at the end,
castle or dungeon. Two stars
form the same stick of ash,
still pointing north.

Of three balls,
only the third is red.
The second's a black mine of untapped vision.
And this one is a leftover moon,
fat as chance.

2. The Game

Not like croquet, where, bleaching on the lawn,
rags become paper and linens straw.
There are ladies who disdain the afternoon
with its theme and variation,
its endless varieties
of the same diamond sandwiches.

Not for them this light
which refracts from a dozen roses
in the slowest dance. Yet they are
meant to be princesses, in the parlor
of elliptical billiards. They will be guided,
cued, and played where they lie,
like caroms, if they remember

that the table is just a string
pulled into the smoke-filled room
by sleight of hand. Isolate a group
of hard-core men
beneath a stained glass lamp.
A bridge of fingertips and wrists could claim them.

   3. The Set

In the left wing of Alzheimer patients
a chair must be only a chair,
the walls blank
lest someone reach out and pick
a wallflower.

There are accidents that want to happen.
But here the light insists
without preference.

If ladies are mentioned again, allow them to stand
on the fringe of the sodden room,
let them wear black. Their hats could be the lamps
that tip off their opponents, their silences
the stocks we sold yesterday.

4. The Cue Ball

A rough sphere laid aside
for months to dry, chiseled smooth
as petrified wood. A golem.
The whitest ball wears a black spot,
a sun spot, a withering glance.

5. Angles of Loss

At any angle the sun declines.
We can drive our balls to their rubber rebound
and drive again. Glass in this place
is thick enough to swallow the stems
of a few false flowers. The light is low.

Stay close to a girl in black with breasts pushed
almost out of her low-cut neckline
and legs that end in smoke.
Let her skin be the cue.
Everyone wins here.

This ball began as a particle
and ended as a wave. It was pocketed.
Define miracle. Grass is just a graph of water.

The solid ivory balls click, revolve,
and click again--like clocks
photographers once used
to exact their visual birds of prey.

SUMMERING

Beethoven's clay bust
falls asleep.
On top of the piano
there's a rock
covered in dust.

When he wakes
it's dusk. The dirty daisies
lift their heads
and the toad hops
into a chamber pot.

Tonight it's his job to wash,
so he takes his food-encrusted
plates across the road
to a spigot, and begins
rinsing.

Around his ears
the insects buzz,
as he stands there,
measuring one note
against the other,

making cloth
out of the water
streaming in feathers
across his thick fingers,
his ugly hands.

THE VIOLIN MARK

At the simplest level, it was a bruise,
a tattoo laid down with great difficulty
against the triangle of a woman's neck.

In this practice room,
a bulky piece of wood under my neck,
I listen to the metronome.
It thinks it's a bird and keeps making
the same chirp over and over, while its eye
moves from place to place.

I'm hoarding notes, forcing them
to fall within the slim confines of each measure.
I'm in a French attic with distant relatives downstairs,
using a wooden mute. It looks like another,
larger bridge. Through one window
I can see red-roofed houses,
and the train clacking like a sewing machine,
seaming fields of blueberries
on its way toward Paris.

I haven't absorbed all the ticking.
Part of me is inside, and part keeps spilling out.
Cotton batting, or bandages.
There are treasures in my unlined pockets:
a suede coin purse with compartments,
a roll of strange money.

Cold seeps through a grate.
Along my collarbone the flower I won't be able to prove
for years begins to put down some simple means

of identification.   I know they can hear me,
though I'm a tissue-paper lady,
far away and decades from home.

THE FANTASY

Grains of sunlight.
The frost running down every leaf like a proof,
outlining features. In my sleep I wasn't wrong
for wanting to wander
beneath my own hands, my breath.

A cold room.
Not to stop or go back or change directions
midstream, but to continue, hurrying
onward toward some modal point.
Where I held a name on my tongue

and instantly tasted erasure.
Where my lover asks,
his hands rocking me gently,
what is it, describe it to me,
and I don't turn my face away.

TO SEE SHADOWS

There must be a dark the eyes
have adjusted to, have gained
employment within,
measuring the values
of copper canisters, the stain of a seventh red
in the rhododendron on the sill.
The cook's implements will be upended
in a ceramic vase--one hand-built
instead of thrown. To see shadows as the objects
they are, the cook must acknowledge
the mutation of things: the nub of garlic
using the butcher block
for the little owl of gray it holds,
the towel resting on a counter
only for the way it bleeds into a glass.
Cupboard doors slightly ajar,
oriental verticals opening towards the viewer.
The room, though only the makeshift heart
of a suburban house, asking the unknown guest
to stand first here, then there, noticing
each time how much less of the half-light
is left to chance.

HAMILTON STREET

After I took the music apart
measure by measure,
I retired to this apartment-sized living room
with a cup of tea,
to peruse that corner of the universe
where one or another star
is discovered
by partial eclipse.

There were crickets singing in the walls.
Also, a dry scratching--
Jan's mouse, a pet
she found under the element
of the gas stove, a baby
that lived on nothing
between dry wall and dreams.

I picked up a roach motel,
a can of sterno,
the makings for green spaghetti,
and came back home
to find my old mattress
on the floor, stained with flowers.

But the worst part was literal--
an old, unwanted pregnancy, and whose was it?
Piles of laundry balanced precariously
on a hand-me-down chair.
Mildew bloomed in the shower.

I woke to the touch tone phone
stuffed under a pillow, the key

secreted in the false belly of a stone,
the head of lettuce hiding its unwashed leaves.

And walked down this short stack of stairs
to open a heavy, insulated door
on the argument--same-old same-old,
that knowledge never changes.

THE BIRDWOMEN DISCUSS UGLY BEAUTY

While we are alone here
on this tableau of island
there is still time
to rescue our household objects.

These lowly and forgotten creamers,
broken pitchers, pots and pans
donated by our mothers--
all enhance the empty shells lying on their backs
in the sand. A lemon on a white plate,
a bodice of brightness,
and the hand of a man
who has arrived too late
are just a few of the fragments
that pose for our pleasure.

In the half-light of dawn
or dusk we lie in the arms
of a pink chair, worn and discarded.
Colors we can't find in our dreams
besiege us daily. It isn't as they think,
when they picture our songs. No,
we recline in the patina of age

with the broken gadgets of civilization
welling up at our feet,
the dark line of a wave
lending itself to foam. Everything we own
has been found painstakingly:
the miscellany of weather,
the details of a dried fish
feathering a rock.

We are beginning to be happy.
We will settle for any fruit
except the orange,
which is perfectly round.

UNDER ZEUS

The first law is thunder, that makes
our hearts lodge in our throats,

forces us up and out of our wooden houses
to witness the first rains of August.

I was alone, dwelling in order. They say the infant
can decipher sounds when it enters the world.

Then these drops, following so closely after chaos,
must be lullabies.

I can still remember his voice. It was the incarnation
of a threat made good. We hid

behind our smiles; our beds were numbered
beside his own. There was a study

with a slatted door. Mother had a rolling pin.
She pleated pastry with her fingers, but he

was unpredictable. The multiplication
of fear is always more fear; we jumped

up and down as children in order to learn this.
I would like to stop referencing him, to cease telling

his story of petulance. But I see through a crease in sky
to where he was once bound with a hundred thongs

of rawhide, only to be freed by a creature
with a hundred hands.

GOURDS

Because they are essentially useless
except for decoration, I think of them
again tonight while you sprawl on the couch
in TV snow, sleep off another difficult day
that began too early, light breaking through
your privacy window to spread its fan. They are virtuosos
of variety--dawn, our love life, these gourds.
I am lifting foliage like a skirt, to determine
what it was worth, our arguments over money
and the child; the harsh armor you've amassed
these recent months. What for? And how beautifully
conceived, I want to say, both remarks framed
with flowers. Their dimpled cups of scent
are not more surprising than the stage-black veins
of the eggplant, whose hidden domes are comelier,
more regular, than the oversexed gourds. Here and there
next season's ornaments have found a niche too early, inserted
their fruits between wires meant to train vines. The same old
round peg in a square hole, only cinched as if it were flesh,
with a second waist squeezed from nothing. The fence itself
cycling around, masking an unsightly sewer
from visitors.

        If I stand again, in memory, before
this shrine, where the inedible fruit meets its purpose
and begins to thrive, white-skinned among so many broad-
leafed versions, or cave in cartoon-like, and face abandonment
while the moon hides beneath leaves of darkness,
and shines there, will there be a way to ease sleep
away from its next victim? Next door a blue light kills
insects all night long, with a sound so regular

it's almost comforting. And I know you will wake up close to morning, turn off the TV, and come upstairs. How you will arrange your body between the sheets.

WHOLE NOTE

The bonfires are beginning on shore.
In ragged clusters sophomoric skaters bring their hands
back to life. Soon the ice

will open like a manhole
and the figure from our past
will tumble in with his hockey stick.

You'll have to creep toward him
on your hands and knees, lay down your coat,
and spread your weight evenly

across the ice. With wind chill, it will be minus forty.
Pam will call the ambulance. By the time it comes
you'll have him--his body attached to yours by the wooden stick.

The puck will sink to the bottom,
floating down through scarves of seaweed
to come to rest in silt like a strange fish.

At the edge of the lake, in one unfrozen corner,
the last duck left in this hemisphere will paddle harder
with naked webbed toes, to keep a small oval of water in motion.

THE PROBLEM OF A HORSE WITHOUT WATER

Whatever escaped the angle
between board and spigot
fell in petal-sized gasps, to fuel
the rough weeds and wild roses.

Replace the horse and it vanishes.
Each time to resurface
inside the pastoral, to pull the plug out
of the bathtub itself. I imagine
water will desert us
the same way the fishes have,
and rise again, with a fresh scent.

A dusty old man
adds his voice to the scenario,
saying *She smells the running water.*
She wants it more than what's
in her trough.

He enters a cardboard shack
and emerges smelling of leather.
He carries a gleaming bucket
slit across the bottom.
In a world like this,
the horse wants so purely.

She licks our hands, the board,
the hidden fungus of the fescue grass,
and when her fur tongue
touches the back of my hand
it is how silently insistent.

MIDDAY

The tasks have been relegated
to their machines, darks and lights,
plates and cups.
If fatigue doesn't overcome me
I might steady myself in the eye of a storm,
lean into the aura
of small things breaking ground.

There must be a halfway point,
a house where women wait on stairs
to eke their way up from the bottom,
dirty children in tow,
the body breathing in and out
only because it doesn't have to think.

If there is a fulcrum
beyond which the future becomes easy,
our age finally the number
we don't resist, then
we have passed it.
I write to you from a place
where chaos is music,
its multiple identities
and incarnations
reduced to a single face,

that of a woman in siesta,
hat tipped, a bowl of deepest calm,
her lips stained with sun.

NOTES:

"Filo" was inspired by the epigraph "The filo, the thread that Mozart follows, is so dependent upon the right beginning...," from *The Life of Mozart* by Alfred Einstein.

"Tinnitus" is dedicated to Ellen Laufer.

"Beethoven and the Birds" was inspired by a line from Beethoven's letter to his doctor friend Wegeler, written in 1801: "...for two years I have avoided almost all social gatherings because it is impossible for me to say to people: "I am deaf.""

"The Strads" relies on details of Stradivarius' life as described in *Antonio Stradivarius, His Life and Work*, by Hill, Hill, and Hill. The term "seccadour" refers to the roof of the house where linen, fruits, and violins were dried.

"Without Ceremony" was written for my daughter Lisa on her thirteenth birthday.

"Bird in the Attic Window" is dedicated to Win Skillman.

"The Birdwomen Discuss Ugly Beauty" was inspired by the line "There is beauty in everything, if you have the eye to see it," from Watson's *Composition*.

"Whole Note" recalls an incident on Greenbelt Lake, Maryland in 1971, when Tom Skillman rescued a hockey skater who had fallen through the ice.

"Midday" was written for Linda Andrews.

Judith Skillman was born in Syracuse, New York, and grew up in Greenbelt, Maryland. She holds a Masters Degree in English Literature from the University of Maryland, and has studied Comparative Literature at the University of Washington. Her first book, *Worship of the Visible Spectrum*, received the King County Arts Commission Publication Prize, and was published by *Breitenbush Books* in 1988. In 1991 she received a Writer's Fellowship from the Washington State Arts Commission. She lives in Bellevue, Washington with her husband and three children.

ABOUT THE ARTIST:

Priscilla Maynard lives in Bellevue, Washington. An artist who has explored and taught in many media, Maynard has been working in Sumi on rice paper for over fifteen years. Sumi, she says, "is the most spontaneous, direct, soulful and soul fulfilling of all media for me."

Priscilla Maynard has exhibited nationally and in the Northwest. Her work can be regularly seen at Foster/White Gallery, Kirkland; major collections include Robert Jeoffrey, Carl Bretten, The Northwest Watercolor Society, Nordstrom's and Rainier Bank.

Her degrees include M.F.A. in Painting and Art History from the University of Iowa, and B.F.A. in Painting from Wesleyan Conservatory.